EL DORADO COUNTY LIBRARY

3 1738 00862 2423

D0754386

This Book Donated to
the Children of Placerville by
Mr. Gordon Purdy
Who Loved Children and
Books in That Order -
Usually.

EL DORADO COUNTY LIBRARY
345 FAIR LANE
PLACERVILLE, CA 95667

Hernán
Cortés

Kristin Petrie

El Dorado County Library
345 Fair Lane
Placerville, CA 95667

visit us at
www.abdopub.com

Published by ABDO Publishing Company, 4940 Viking Drive, Edina, Minnesota 55435. Copyright © 2004 by Abdo Consulting Group, Inc. International copyrights reserved in all countries. No part of this book may be reproduced in any form without written permission from the publisher.

Printed in the United States.

Cover Photos: Corbis
Interior Photos: Corbis pp. 4, 5, 7, 8, 9, 10, 11, 13, 15, 16, 17, 19, 23, 24, 25, 26, 27, 29

Series Coordinator: Stephanie Hedlund
Editors: Kate A. Conley, Kristin Van Cleaf
Art Direction & Cover Design: Neil Klinepier
Interior Design & Maps: Dave Bullen

Library of Congress Cataloging-in-Publication Data

Petrie, Kristin, 1970-
    Hernán Cortés / Kristin Petrie.
        p. cm. -- (Explorers)
    Summary: An introduction to the life of Hernando Cortés, the Spanish explorer who discovered Baja California and explored the Pacific coast of Mexico, but who is best remembered for conquering the Aztec Empire.
    Includes bibliographical references and index.
    ISBN 1-59197-598-0
    1. Cortâs, Hernân, 1485-1547--Juvenile literature. 2. Mexico--Discovery and exploration--Spanish--Juvenile literature. 3. Mexico--History--Conquest, 1519-1540--Juvenile literature. 4. Explorers--Mexico--Biography--Juvenile literature. 5. Explorers--Spain--Biography--Juvenile literature. 6. Conquerors--Mexico--Biography--Juvenile literature. [1. Cortâs, Hernando, 1485-1547. 2. Explorers. 3. Mexico--Discovery and exploration. 4. Mexico--History--Conquest, 1519-1540.] I. Title.

F1230.C835P475 2004
972'.02'092--dc22
    [B]   2003066531

Contents

4

Hernán Cortés

During the 1500s, Spain was a powerful nation in the Old World. **Civil wars** had ended. Spanish forces had finally conquered the Moors, the North African warriors who had **oppressed** Spaniards for centuries. And, Spanish explorers had found a New World.

Spain was ready to conquer this New World. Hernán Cortés was one of the men to do it. This daring man was a conquistador, which is a Spanish explorer and conqueror. He led his men to battle against 100,000 or more natives.

Conquistadors claimed much of the New World for Spain.

	1451 Christopher Columbus born		1485 Hernán Cortés born	
1450 John Cabot born		1460 Vasco da Gama born		1491 Jacques Cartier born

Cortés has been called one of the most courageous military commanders of all time. His victories led to 300 years of Spanish control over Mexico and Central America. Read on to follow Cortés's **conquests**.

Hernán Cortés

1492
Columbus's first voyage west for Spain

1496
Cabot's first voyage for England

1493
Columbus's second voyage, attempted to colonize Hispaniola

Early Years

Hernán Cortés was born in Medellín, Spain, in 1485. Medellín was in Extremadura, the poorest **province** in Spain. Life there provided few opportunities to make a living. This made many young men become soldiers. They hoped to be sent to foreign lands, where they might find riches.

Hernán's parents were Martín Cortés de Monroy and Catalina Pizarro Altamarino. Martín was an **infantry** officer. He and his wife were of minor nobility and were well respected. The Cortés family was neither rich nor poor, but they were very proud.

Hernán's family saved enough money to send him to a university in Salamanca, Spain. When he was just 14 years old, Hernán went there to study Latin and law. The young boy, however, was restless.

To his parents' disappointment, Hernán returned home after only two years. Back in Medellín, he became bored and began looking for an opportunity to leave Spain.

1497
Cabot's second voyage, discovered the Grand Banks; da Gama was first to sail around Africa to India

1496 or 1497
Hernando de Soto born

1498
Cabot's third voyage, may have died; Columbus's third voyage

Would You?

Would you have returned to the poorest province? Or, would you have stayed at the university to begin a career? Why do you think Cortés returned home?

This monument marks the home where Hernán Cortés was born.

1502
Columbus's fourth voyage; da Gama's second voyage

1506
Columbus died

1504
Cortés sailed to the West Indies

Across the Ocean

In 1492, Christopher Columbus had claimed new territory for Spain across the Atlantic Ocean. Hernán dreamed of sailing there. He longed for any excitement, wealth, and glory that might be found in the New World.

In 1504, Hernán's dream came true. The 19-year-old boarded a ship to the West Indies. After a long and difficult voyage, the ship docked in the port town of Santo Domingo, Hispaniola.

Because Hernán was a nobleman, he was immediately offered land. But Hernán hadn't come to farm, he had come to search for gold! The settlement was so new, however, there was little else to do. He farmed for seven years, but he was always dreaming of adventure.

Santo Domingo

1511
Cortés helped take over Cuba

1510
Francisco Vásquez de Coronado born

1514
De Soto went to the New World

Would you follow your dream into the unknown New World? What do you imagine the trip across the Atlantic Ocean was like?

Hernán Cortés suffered from poor health for most of his life. In Santo Domingo, his health kept him from participating in expeditions to South America in 1509. It also forced him to farm in Santo Domingo for longer than he wanted.

Conquering Cuba

Hernán's adventure presented itself in 1511. By then, Spain had claimed a large area of land in the New World. Yet the Spaniards wanted more. They wanted to take over the fertile lands of Cuba. Diego Velázquez, a wealthy landowner in Hispaniola, led this mission in 1511. Hernán joined his forces.

Conquering the natives in Cuba was easy for the Spaniards. Velázquez was made governor of the new Spanish colony.

The coastline of Cuba, which Cortés helped conquer

Hernán was given land and slaves. He began raising livestock on a large new ranch.

Hernán met and married a Spanish woman in Cuba. Catalina Xuárez was a relative of Governor Velázquez. Catalina and Hernán did not have children.

1524
Da Gama's third voyage, died in Cochin, India

1519–1521
Cortés conquered the Aztec Empire and claimed Mexico for Spain

1532
De Soto helped attack the Inca Empire

In Cuba, Hernán became wealthy. He had a large home, new wife, and prosperous ranch. Still, he was not satisfied. He continued to have adventure on his mind.

A bust of Hernán Cortés

Would You?

Would you join an expedition to conquer a new land? What do you think the natives thought of the Spaniards?

The Expedition

Cortés's next adventure was brought about by events in 1517. In that year, Spaniard Francisco Fernández de Córdoba was blown off his sea course while looking for slaves.

Fernández de Córdoba landed on the Yucatán **Peninsula**, on the eastern side of today's Mexico. The captain was astonished by what he saw.

On this peninsula were entire cities built of stone. The natives wore cotton clothes of bright colors. They appeared to be highly civilized. This was the first developed society the Spaniards had found in the New World. The captain had stumbled into the center of the **Mayan** civilization.

When Velázquez heard of this discovery, he sent out a small expedition to gather more information. They learned that the Maya lived on a large landmass, not another tiny island. This new landmass was said to contain cities full of gold.

1534
Cartier's first voyage for France

1539–1542
De Soto explored La Florida

1533
De Soto helped take over Cuzco

1535
Cartier's second voyage

The Mayan civilization began around 1500 BC. By AD 200, the Maya had built cities, temples, pyramids, and palaces. The Mayan ruin Palenque was first discovered in 1784. It is still visited today.

Governor Velázquez decided to send an expedition to the **peninsula**. He made Hernán Cortés its leader. Cortés jumped at the opportunity.

Cortés was so excited, he spent excessive amounts of money in preparation for the mission. This eagerness started to worry the governor. Was the ambitious Spaniard going to claim all of the new land, riches, and power for himself?

Velázquez attempted to cancel the expedition. He no longer wanted Cortés to be in charge. Cortés heard about the governor's plans and slipped away to one of his ships. By avoiding Velázquez's men, he couldn't be served the papers that released him of his duty.

Cortés continued to organize his expedition from the waters off the coast of Cuba. On February 10, 1519, Commander Cortés and his **fleet** set sail. The 11 ships containing 16 horses, 100 sailors, and 508 soldiers headed for present-day Mexico.

1541
Cartier's third voyage, attempted to colonize Canada; Cortés volunteered to fight against Algiers

1540
Coronado set out to find the Seven Cities of Cíbola; Francis Drake born

Cortés's fleet leaving Cuba

1547
Cortés died

1557
Cartier died

1542
Coronado returned to New Spain; de Soto died

1554
Coronado died

1566
Drake's first voyage to the New World

Mexico

Cortés soon landed on Cozumel, a Mexican island. There, the Spaniards **subdued** the natives and began converting them to Christianity. Cortés also located a Spaniard on the island.

A beach on Cozumel, Mexico

Jerónimo de Aguilar had been shipwrecked on Cozumel eight years earlier. Since then, he had been a servant to the native **Maya**. Because he knew the Mayan language, Aguilar became an interpreter for Cortés.

From Cozumel, Cortés sailed to the mainland and landed at the town of Tabasco. The Tabascans defended their city bravely. But, they were no match for the Spaniards' guns and **ammunition**.

1567
Drake's second voyage

1577
Drake began a worldwide voyage, was first Englishman to sail the Pacific Ocean

1570 and 1572
Drake terrorized the Spanish in the New World

After the battle, the natives presented 20 women to Cortés as a peace offering. Among them was a woman named Marina.

Marina became an important part of the expedition. She spoke several languages and became an interpreter for Cortés. The Tabascan woman also told Cortés about native **customs**.

On Cozumel, Aguilar may have lived in a Mayan hut similar to this one.

The Aztecs

Cortés continued sailing along the coast. In April 1519, he boldly decided to form his own settlement on the southeastern Mexican coast. He named it Veracruz.

Cortés took the title captain general of the new settlement. He resigned as commander of Velázquez's expedition. He claimed he worked directly for the king of Spain. Under Spanish law, these actions gave Cortés the authority to conquer all of Mexico.

In Veracruz, Cortés heard about another native tribe, the **Aztecs**. Marina and Aguilar translated for Cortés. Marina translated from Nahuatl, the Aztecan language, to **Mayan**. Aguilar translated from Mayan to Spanish. In this way, Cortés and his men learned about the Aztecs.

The Spaniards were told about the Aztec Empire's capital, Tenochtitlán. They also learned about the Aztecan religion. Cortés was informed that the area tribes were forced to

1588
Drake helped England win the Battle of Gravelines against Spain's Invincible Armada

1581
Drake knighted by Queen Elizabeth I

1596
Drake died

provide the **Aztecs** human offerings and pay taxes.

Cortés used the information he gathered to his advantage. Through Marina and Aguilar he convinced the native tribes to fight with him against the Aztecs. He knew he needed these **allies** if he wanted to conquer the empire.

The Aztecan capital Tenochtitlán was on an island in Lake Texcoco.

Would you trust the native tribes to fight against the Aztecs? Do you think Cortés feared the natives?

1728
James Cook born

1734
Daniel Boone born

1765
Boone journeyed to Florida

1767
Boone explored Kentucky

1768
Cook sailed for Tahiti

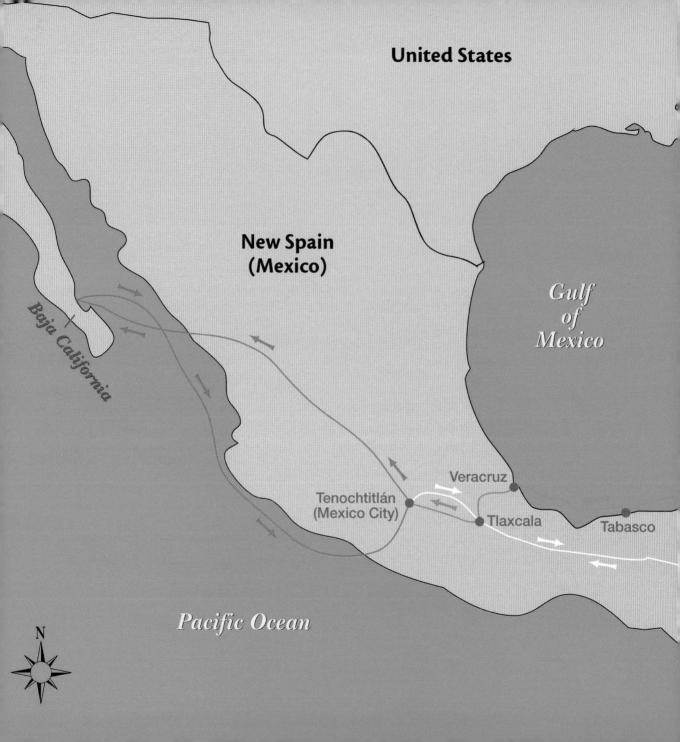

United States

New Spain
(Mexico)

Gulf
of
Mexico

Baja California

Veracruz

Tenochtitlán
(Mexico City)

Tlaxcala

Tabasco

Pacific Ocean

N

The Journeys of Hernán Cortés

1519 TO 1521 →	───
1524 TO 1526 →	───
1535 TO 1536 →	───

Atlantic Ocean

Cuba

Santiago de Cuba

Yucatán Peninsula

Cozumel

Caribbean Sea

Hispaniola

Honduras

Tenochtitlán

In August 1519, the Spaniards and thousands of **allied** natives began their march toward Tenochtitlán. Cortés reached the capital city in November. Emperor Montezuma II decided to let him enter.

Montezuma II showed the Spaniards his empire. The streets, palaces, and parks amazed them. The city even had a zoo. They were horrified, however, by the many temples where human sacrifices took place.

Cortés had a small army compared to the **Aztecs**. He knew he could not conquer them by force. So, he took Montezuma II **hostage** and began ruling the people of Tenochtitlán through the emperor.

While it seemed an easy **conquest**, Cortés actually had been lucky. Montezuma II thought Cortés was the god Quetzalcoatl. This and other **omens** had led the emperor to believe the gods had chosen to end the Aztecs' empire.

Cortés finally had glory and power. He and his soldiers stayed in palaces. They were escorted around the city by the emperor himself.

Cortés meeting Montezuma II

QUETZALCOATL
● ● ●

Quetzalcoatl was an Aztecan god. His name means "feathered serpent" in the Nahuatl language.

Quetzalcoatl was the patron of priests and the inventor of the calendar. He was also the morning and evening star.

The Aztecs' lands were first ruled by the Toltecs. They had expelled Quetzalcoatl from their capital. However, it was said he would return.

The Aztecs believed the god would take the form of a man with a beard. Montezuma II thought the bearded Cortés was Quetzalcoatl returning to destroy the Aztecs.

1778
Cook became the first European to record Hawaiian Islands; Boone captured by Shawnee

1775
Boone cut the Wilderness Road from Virginia to Kentucky

1779
Cook died

The Conquest

About six months after taking over Tenochtitlán, Cortés heard that more Spaniards had arrived in the region. Velázquez had sent Pánfilo de Narváez to remove Cortés from power.

After a storm one night, Cortés led a surprise attack on the large army. He captured Narváez without difficulty. Following this, Cortés easily persuaded the troops to join him.

Pedro de Alvarado

Back in Tenochtitlán, Commander Pedro de Alvarado had been left in charge. There had been tension during Cortés's absence. Alvarado allowed the citizens to hold a religious festival. Then, he ordered his men to fire on them. The **Aztecs** fought back, and the Spaniards fled to their palace.

1813
John C. Frémont born

1842
Frémont's first independent surveying mission

1820
Boone died

When Cortés returned to the city, **Aztecan** soldiers still surrounded the palace. Montezuma II was sent to speak to them, but they no longer followed his command. The emperor died after being stoned by his own people.

The stoning of Montezuma II

In June 1520, the Spaniards attempted to sneak out of the city. More than 600 Spaniards died on this night, which is still called "the night of tears." Only Cortés and a small group managed to cross the lake to safety. They rested during the remainder of the year in the region of the Tlaxcalans.

1856
Frémont ran for president of the United States but lost

1845-1846
Frémont explored the Great Basin and the Pacific Coast, fought in the Mexican War

1890
Frémont died

Exploring Further

Cortés again gathered thousands of native **allies**. His army renewed, he planned to take over Tenochtitlán once again. Cortés began a siege on the city in December 1520. It lasted more than seven months. Finally, on August 13, 1521, the **Aztecs** surrendered.

Cortés was named governor and captain general of the territory. He tore down Tenochtitlán and built Mexico City.

His wife, Catalina, joined him there but died soon after arriving. Cortés began longing for the next adventure.

Cortés began sending expeditions to explore New Spain. In 1524, he joined one of these expeditions. On this two-year journey, he and an army struggled through thick rain forests and eventually reached what is now Honduras.

Charles I granted Cortés this coat of arms

1910
Jacques Cousteau born

1951
Cousteau's first expedition in the Red Sea

1942
Cousteau and Gagnan developed the Aqua-Lung for diving

During Cortés's absence, King Charles I had been convinced to take away his titles. So, Cortés returned to Spain in 1528. He was greeted with much **fanfare**. He had, after all, sent vast amounts of gold and other treasures to Spain over the years.

Cortés's return to Mexico after his Honduras expedition

Would you give Cortés back the title of governor? Why do you think King Charles I took it away in the first place?

Last Adventures

While in Spain, King Charles I renewed Cortés's title as captain general of New Spain. And, Cortés married a noblewoman named Juana de Zuñiga. He and his new wife returned to Mexico in 1530.

In 1535, Cortés set out to find the legendary Seven Cities of Cíbola. He reached present-day Baja California, Mexico, and attempted to establish a colony. He failed and returned to Mexico City in 1536.

Cortés continued to search for riches in New Spain. He sent several expeditions through northwestern Mexico, but they found nothing. These failed explorations cost Cortés a lot of money. He went into **debt** after the expensive travels.

Determined to continue exploring, Cortés decided to ask King Charles I for help. Cortés went to Spain in 1540, but the king was at war in Algiers. Cortés volunteered to serve in the war in 1541.

1997
Cousteau died

1974
Cousteau formed the Cousteau Society to protect marine life

Later, Hernán Cortés fell ill in Seville, Spain, and died there on December 2, 1547. Cortés contributed much to the New World. He introduced Spain to Mexico. The native and Spanish **cultures** were joined by his arrival. Cortés helped establish the Mexican culture that lives today.

This memorial to Cortés stands in Medellín, Spain.

Glossary

allies - people or countries that agree to help each other in times of need.

ammunition - bullets, shells, and other items used in firearms.

Aztec - a native people of Mexico. The Aztecs ruled a large empire in the 1400s and 1500s until they were conquered by the Spaniards.

civil war - a war between groups in the same country.

conquest - the act of conquering.

culture - the customs, arts, and tools of a nation or people at a certain time.

customs - the habits of a group that are passed on through generations.

debt - something owed to someone, usually money.

fanfare - showy outward display.

fleet - a group of ships under one command.

hostage - a person held captive by another person or group in order to make a deal with authorities or control a situation.

infantry - soldiers trained and organized to fight on foot.

Maya - a native people of Central America and Mexico. The Mayan civilization flourished from the 200s to the 800s. It declined long before being discovered by the Spaniards.

omen - something that is believed to foretell a future event.

oppress - to govern harshly or to keep down unjustly or cruelly.

peninsula - land that sticks out into water and is connected to a larger landmass.

province - a geographical or governmental division of a country.

subdue - to bring under control by using force.

John Cabot   *Christopher Columbus*   *Francisco Vásquez de Coronado*

Daniel Boone   *Jacques Cartier*   *James Cook*

conquistador - kahn-KEES-tuh-dawr
Cozumel - koh-soo-MEHL
Diego Velázquez - DYAY-goh bay-LAHTH-kayth
Nahuatl - NAH-wah-tuhl
Pánfilo de Narváez - PAHM-fee-loh thay nahr-BAH-ayth
Pedro de Alvarado - PAY-throh thay ahl-bah-RAHTH-oh
Quetzalcoatl - kweht-suhl-kuh-WAH-tuhl
Tenochtitlán - tay-nawch-teet-LAHN
Yucatán - yoo-kah-TAHN

To learn more about Hernán Cortés, visit ABDO Publishing Company on the World Wide Web at **www.abdopub.com**. Web sites about Hernán Cortés are featured on our Book Links page. These links are routinely monitored and updated to provide the most current information available.

Index

MAR 0 9 2012